BASKETBALL TIME!

by Brendan Flynn

BUMBA BOOKS™

LERNER PUBLICATIONS ◆ MINNEAPOLIS

Note to Educators:

Throughout this book, you'll find critical thinking questions. These can be used to engage young readers in thinking critically about the topic and in using the text and photos to do so.

Lerner Publications Company
A division of Lerner Publishing Group, Inc.
241 First Avenue North
Minneapolis, MN 55401 USA

For reading levels and more information, look up this title at www.lernerbooks.com.

Library of Congress Cataloging-in-Publication Data

Names: Flynn, Brendan, 1977–
Title: Basketball time! / by Brendan Flynn.
Description: Minneapolis : Lerner Publications, [2017] | Series: Bumba books—Sports Time! | Includes bibliographical references and index.
Identifiers: LCCN 2016001062 (print) | LCCN 2016005881 (ebook) | ISBN 9781512414325 (lb : alk. paper) | ISBN 9781512415391 (pb : alk. paper) | ISBN 9781512415407 (eb pdf)
Subjects: LCSH: Basketball—Juvenile literature.
Classification: LCC GV885.1 .F59 2017 (print) | LCC GV885.1 (ebook) | DDC 796.323—dc23

LC record available at http://lccn.loc.gov/2016001062

Manufactured in the United States of America
1 – VP – 7/15/16

Expand learning beyond the printed book. Download free, complementary educational resources for this book from our website, www.lernerresource.com.

Table of **Contents**

We Play Basketball

Basketball is a sport.

Anyone can play.

You can play on a team.

You can play with friends.

hoop

ball

shoes

6

You need a ball.

You need a hoop.

A good pair of shoes helps too.

You can play in a gym.

You can play outside.

You can play in a driveway.

How do you think playing basketball is different outside?

Two teams play

each other.

The area they play on is

called a court.

Each team has a hoop on

one end of the court.

Players bounce the ball.

This is called dribbling.

Players pass the ball to teammates.

They shoot the ball into the hoop.

Why might you pass the ball to a teammate?

The other team tries to

stop them.

They take the ball away.

Then they get a chance

to score a basket.

Each basket is worth points.

Most are worth two points.

Some are worth three points.

The team with the most points wins

the game.

You could see a game at your school.

You could go to an arena.

Many games are on TV.

Where else could you see a basketball game?

Basketball is fun to watch.

It is fun to play too.

Basketball Court

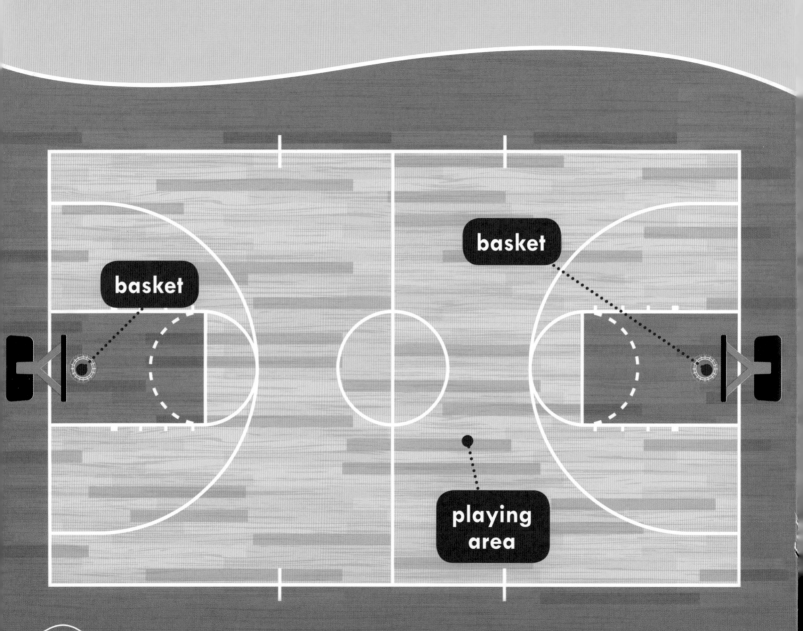

basket

basket

playing area

Picture Glossary

arena

a place where people play and watch sports games

basket

when the ball goes into the hoop

court

an area marked with lines for playing basketball games

dribbling

bouncing the ball up and down

23

Index

Read More

Morey, Allan. *Basketball.* Minneapolis: Jump!, 2015.

Nelson, Robin. *Basketball Is Fun!* Minneapolis: Lerner Publications, 2014.

Tometich, Annabelle. *I Know Basketball.* Ann Arbor, MI: Cherry Lake Publishing, 2013.

Photo Credits

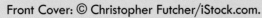